UNCHARTED: STORIES OF SURVIVAL

HEAT WAVE Horror!

by Harriet McGregor

Illustrations by Alan Brown and Diego Viasberg

BEARPORT PUBLISHING

Minneapolis, Minnesota

BEAR CLAW

Credits: 20, © ChameleonsEye/Shutterstock; 21t, © CGN089/Shutterstock; 21b, © Taisya Korchak/Shutterstock; 22, © Anja Ivanovic/Shutterstock; 23, © fotosav/Shutterstock.

Supervising Editor: Allison Juda
Editor: Sarah Eason
Proofreader: Jennifer Sanderson
Designer: Paul Myerscough

DISCLAIMER: This graphic story is a dramatization based on true events. It is intended to give the reader a sense of the narrative rather than a presentation of actual details as they occurred.

Library of Congress Cataloging-in-Publication Data

Names: McGregor, Harriet, author. | Viasberg, Diego, 1981- illustrator. |
  Brown, Alan (Illustrator), illustrator.
Title: Heat wave horror! / by Harriet McGregor ; Illustrations by
  Diego Viasberg, Alan Brown.
Description: Bear claw edition. | Minneapolis, Minnesota : Bearport
  Publishing, [2021] | Series: Uncharted: stories of survival | Includes
  bibliographical references and index.
Identifiers: LCCN 2020008711 (print) | LCCN 2020008712 (ebook) | ISBN
  9781647470333 (library binding) | ISBN 9781647470401 (paperback) | ISBN
  9781647470470 (ebook)
Subjects: LCSH: Heat waves (Meteorology)–Juvenile literature. | Heat waves
  (Meteorology)–Comic books, strips, etc. | Survival–Juvenile
  literature. | Survival–Comic books, strips, etc. | Graphic novels.
Classification: LCC QC981.8.A5 M38 2021 (print) | LCC QC981.8.A5 (ebook)
  | DDC 363.34/92–dc23
LC record available at https://lccn.loc.gov/2020008711
LC ebook record available at https://lccn.loc.gov/2020008712

For more information, write to Bearport Publishing, 5357 Penn Avenue South, Minneapolis, MN 55419. Printed in the United States of America.

CONTENTS

Chapter 1
The Race to Help..................... 4

Chapter 2
Keeping Cool 8

Chapter 3
Sick in the City..................... 12

Chapter 4
Hot Enough to Kill 16

What Is a Heat Wave?.............................. 20

Keep Safe 22

Glossary 23

Index.. 24

Read More 24

Learn More Online 24

Chapter 1

THE RACE TO HELP

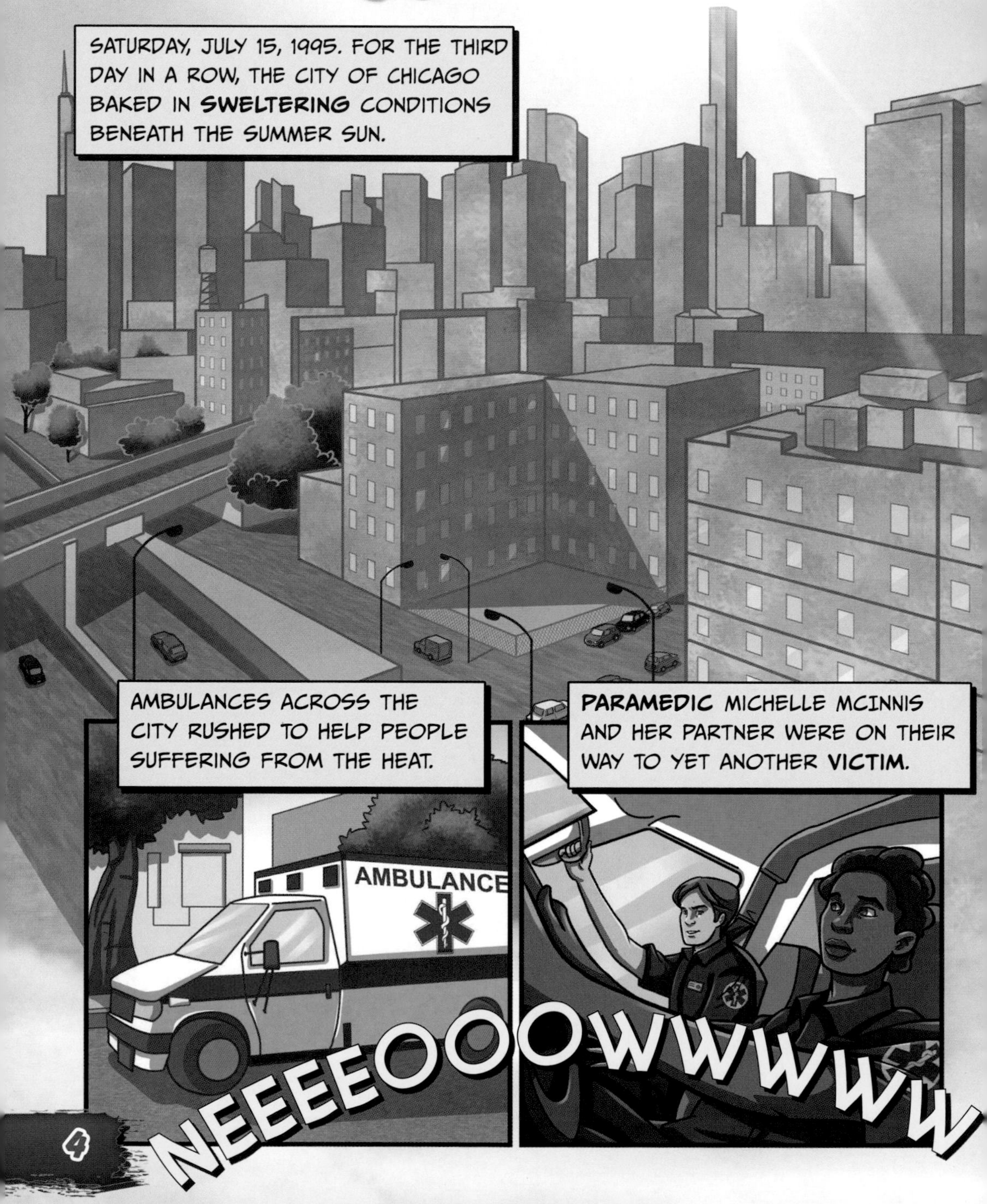

SATURDAY, JULY 15, 1995. FOR THE THIRD DAY IN A ROW, THE CITY OF CHICAGO BAKED IN **SWELTERING** CONDITIONS BENEATH THE SUMMER SUN.
AMBULANCES ACROSS THE CITY RUSHED TO HELP PEOPLE SUFFERING FROM THE HEAT.
PARAMEDIC MICHELLE MCINNIS AND HER PARTNER WERE ON THEIR WAY TO YET ANOTHER **VICTIM.**
AMBULANCE
NEEEEOOOOWWWWWW

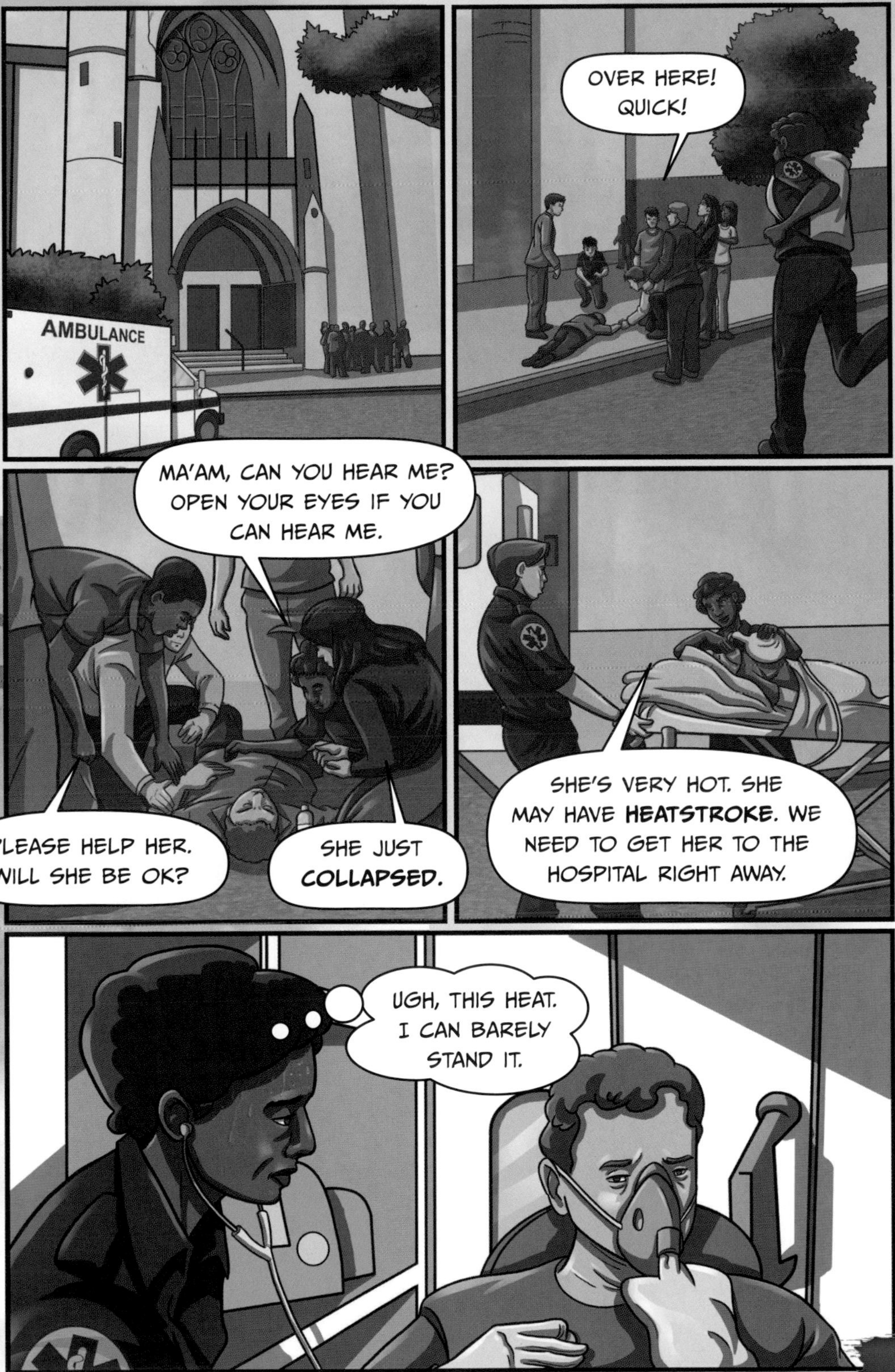
AMBULANCE
OVER HERE! QUICK!
MA'AM, CAN YOU HEAR ME? OPEN YOUR EYES IF YOU CAN HEAR ME.
PLEASE HELP HER. WILL SHE BE OK?
SHE JUST **COLLAPSED.**
SHE'S VERY HOT. SHE MAY HAVE **HEATSTROKE**. WE NEED TO GET HER TO THE HOSPITAL RIGHT AWAY.
UGH, THIS HEAT. I CAN BARELY STAND IT.

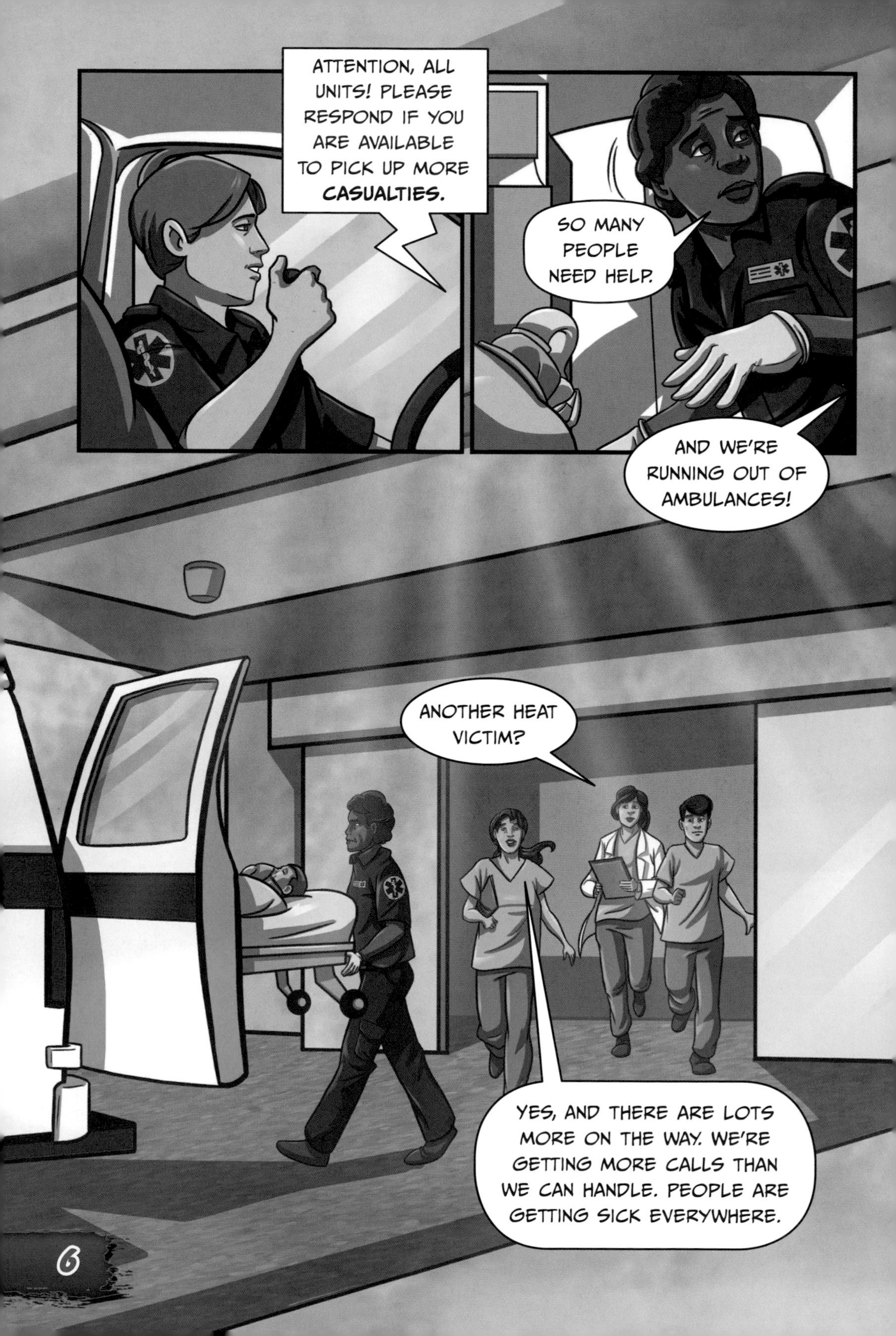
ATTENTION, ALL UNITS! PLEASE RESPOND IF YOU ARE AVAILABLE TO PICK UP MORE CASUALTIES.
SO MANY PEOPLE NEED HELP.
AND WE'RE RUNNING OUT OF AMBULANCES!
ANOTHER HEAT VICTIM?
YES, AND THERE ARE LOTS MORE ON THE WAY. WE'RE GETTING MORE CALLS THAN WE CAN HANDLE. PEOPLE ARE GETTING SICK EVERYWHERE.

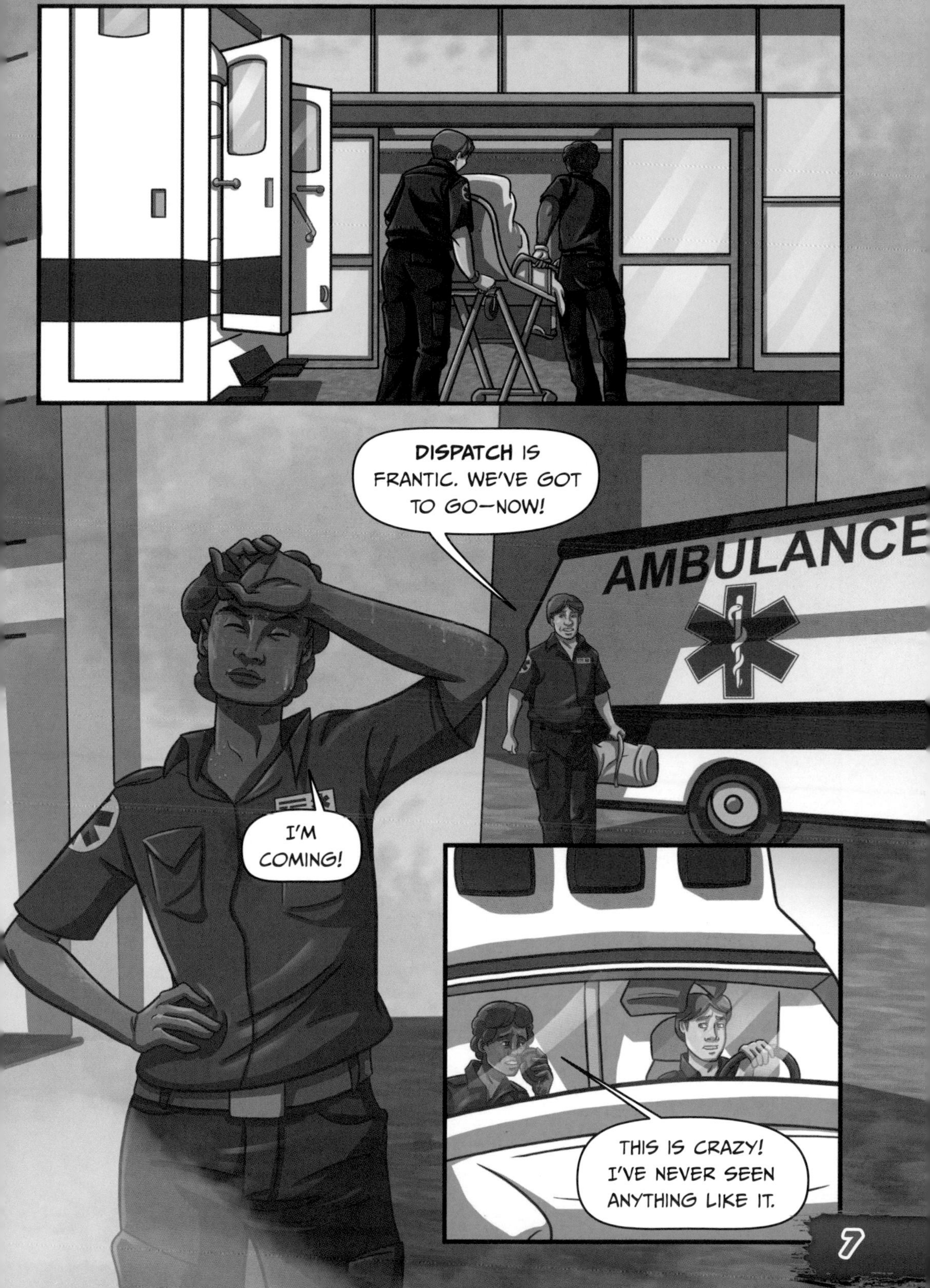
DISPATCH IS FRANTIC. WE'VE GOT TO GO—NOW!
I'M COMING!
AMBULANCE
THIS IS CRAZY! I'VE NEVER SEEN ANYTHING LIKE IT.

Chapter 2

KEEPING COOL

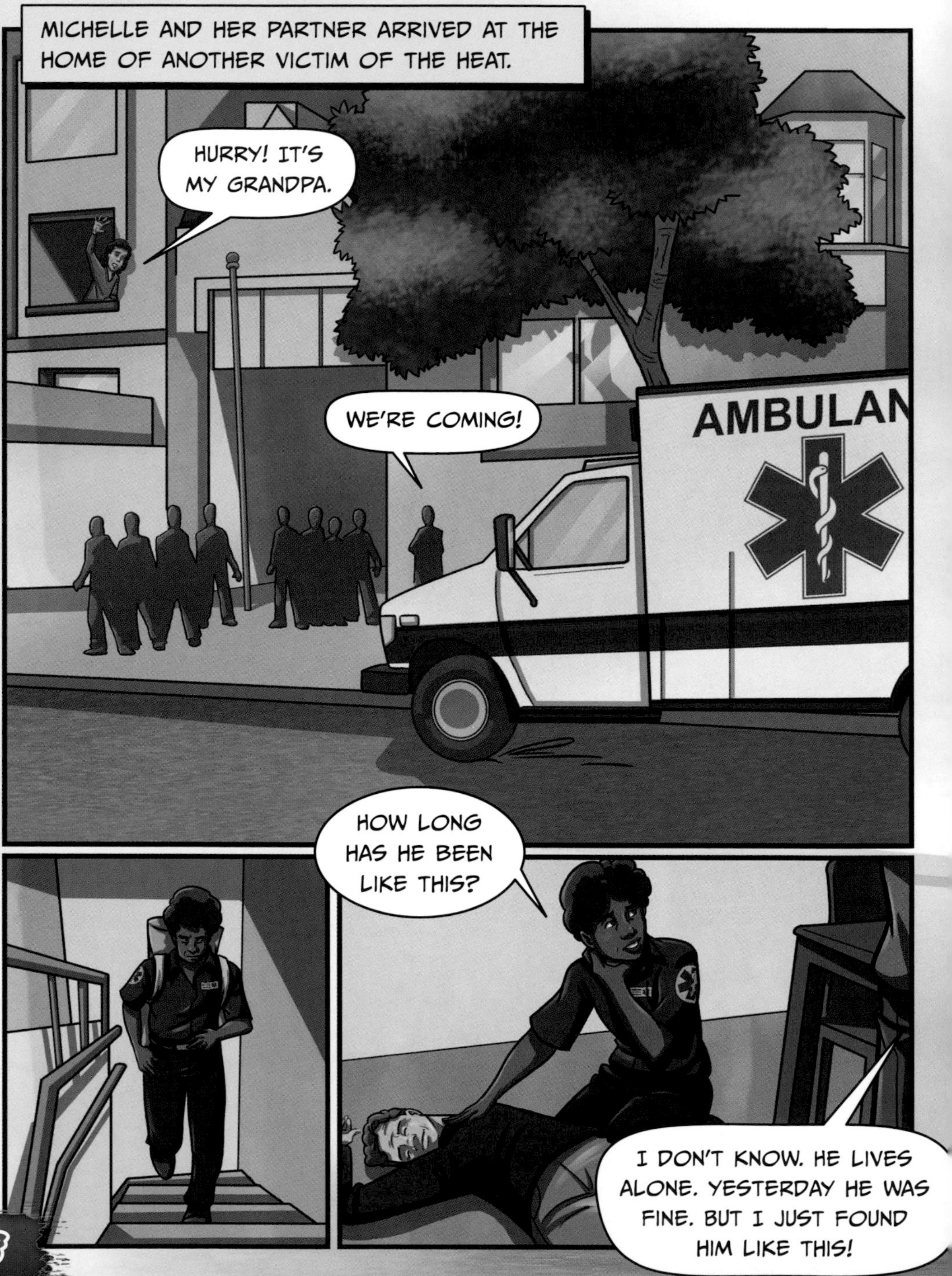

MICHELLE AND HER PARTNER ARRIVED AT THE HOME OF ANOTHER VICTIM OF THE HEAT.
HURRY! IT'S MY GRANDPA.
WE'RE COMING!
AMBULAN
HOW LONG HAS HE BEEN LIKE THIS?
I DON'T KNOW. HE LIVES ALONE. YESTERDAY HE WAS FINE. BUT I JUST FOUND HIM LIKE THIS!

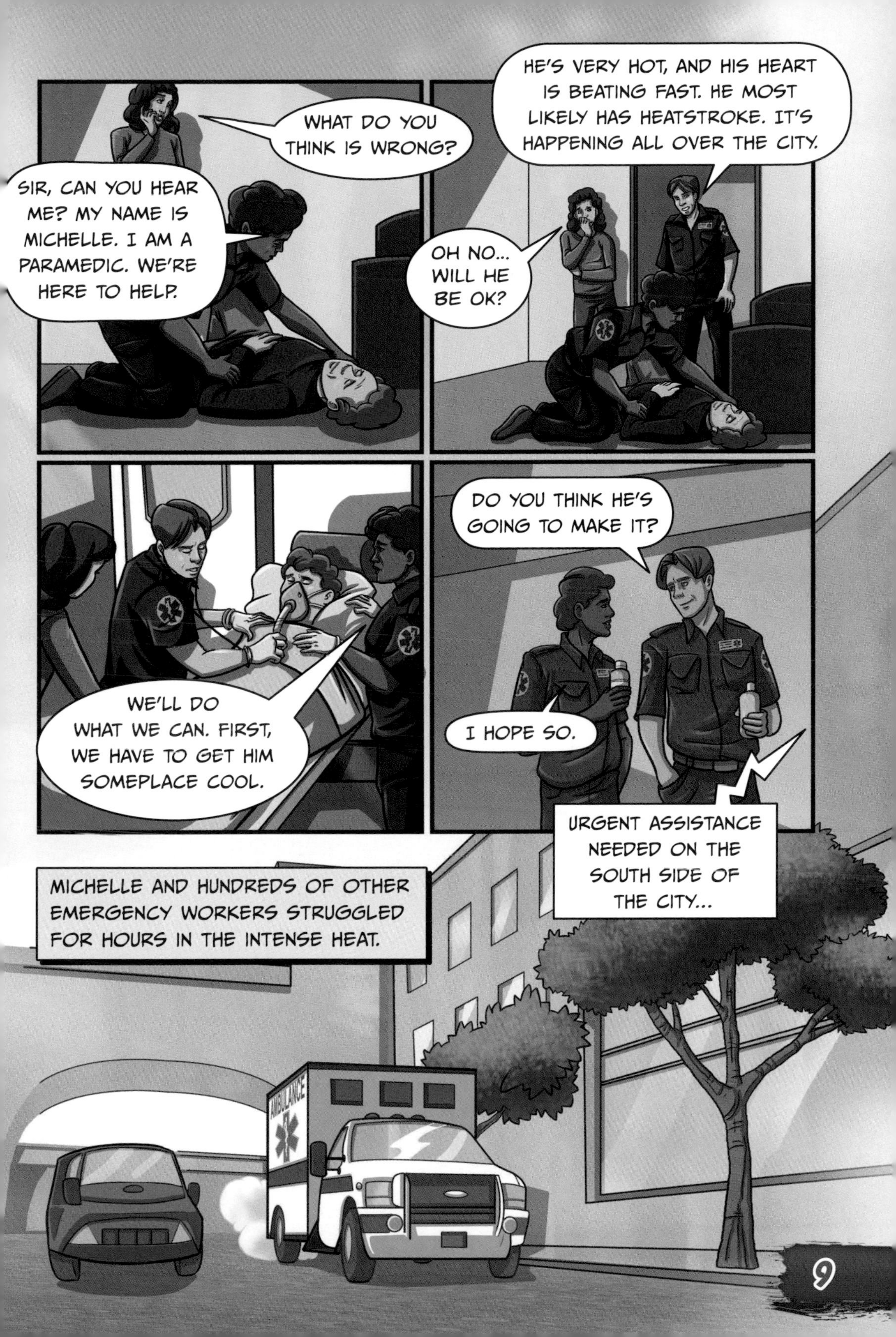
SIR, CAN YOU HEAR ME? MY NAME IS MICHELLE. I AM A PARAMEDIC. WE'RE HERE TO HELP.
WHAT DO YOU THINK IS WRONG?
HE'S VERY HOT, AND HIS HEART IS BEATING FAST. HE MOST LIKELY HAS HEATSTROKE. IT'S HAPPENING ALL OVER THE CITY.
OH NO... WILL HE BE OK?
WE'LL DO WHAT WE CAN. FIRST, WE HAVE TO GET HIM SOMEPLACE COOL.
DO YOU THINK HE'S GOING TO MAKE IT?
I HOPE SO.
URGENT ASSISTANCE NEEDED ON THE SOUTH SIDE OF THE CITY...
MICHELLE AND HUNDREDS OF OTHER EMERGENCY WORKERS STRUGGLED FOR HOURS IN THE INTENSE HEAT.
AMBULANCE

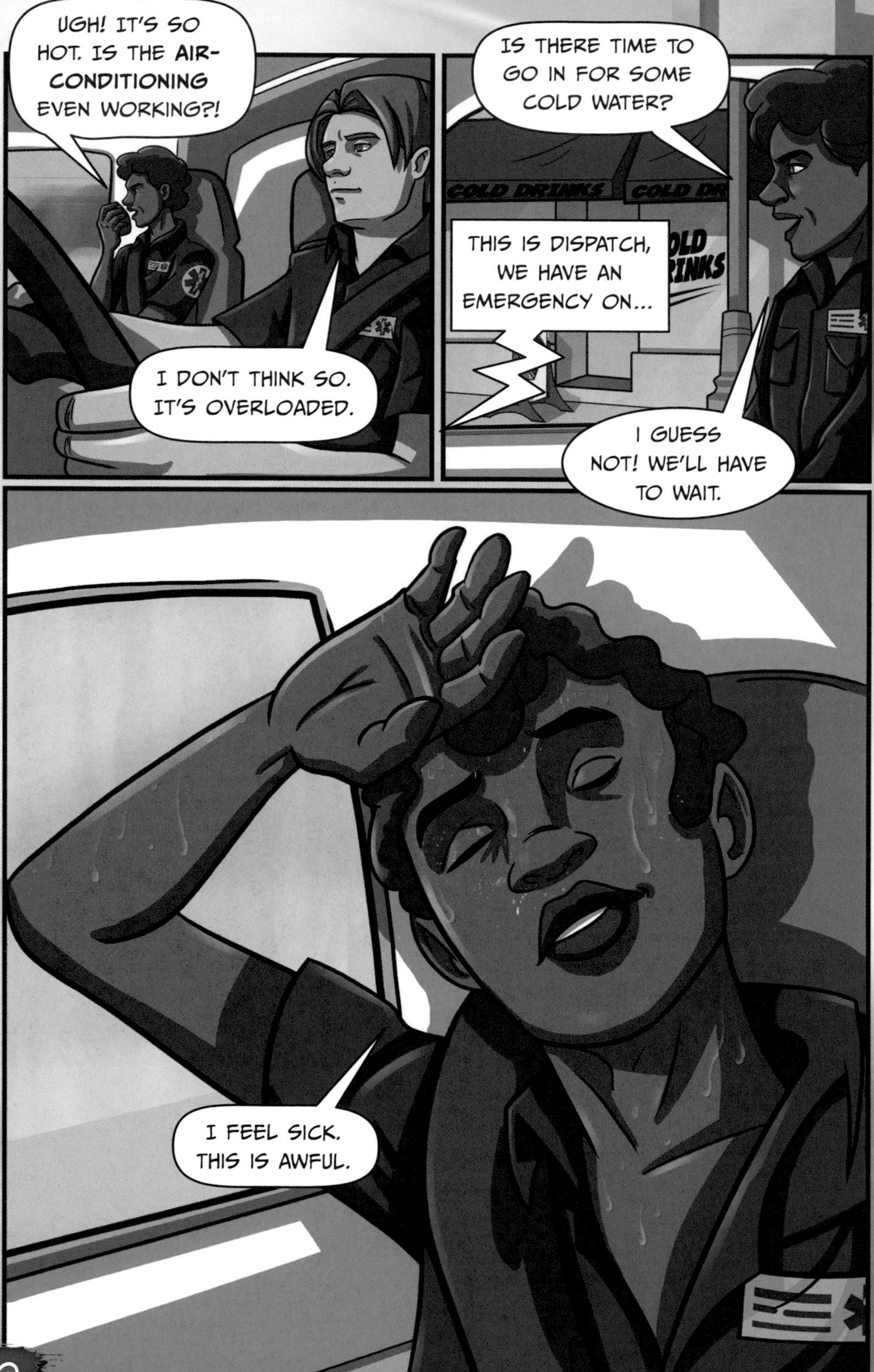
UGH! IT'S SO HOT. IS THE **AIR-CONDITIONING** EVEN WORKING?!
I DON'T THINK SO. IT'S OVERLOADED.
IS THERE TIME TO GO IN FOR SOME COLD WATER?
COLD DRINKS
THIS IS DISPATCH, WE HAVE AN EMERGENCY ON...
I GUESS NOT! WE'LL HAVE TO WAIT.
I FEEL SICK. THIS IS AWFUL.

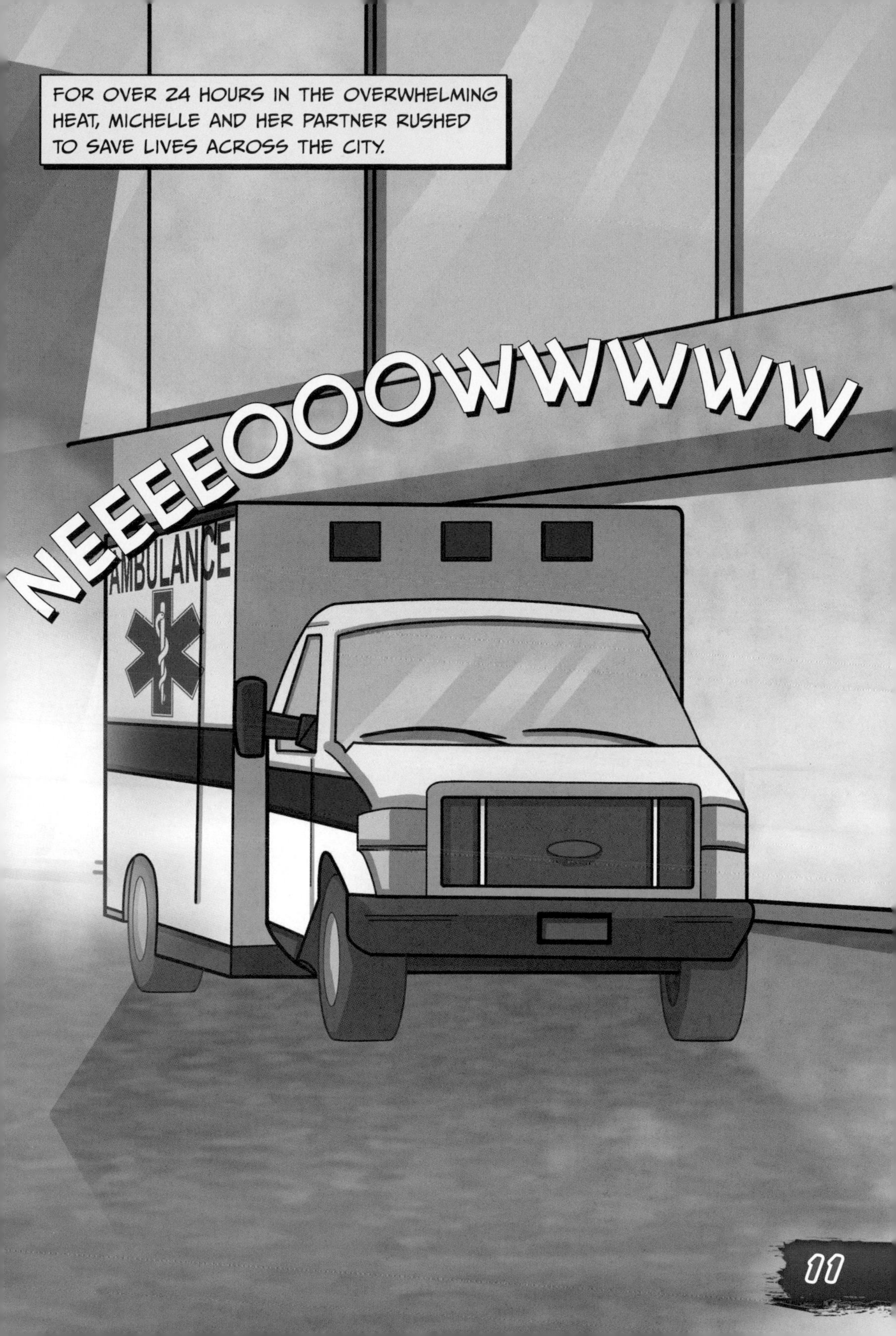
FOR OVER 24 HOURS IN THE OVERWHELMING HEAT, MICHELLE AND HER PARTNER RUSHED TO SAVE LIVES ACROSS THE CITY.
NEEEEOOOOWWWWW
AMBULANCE

Chapter 3

SICK IN THE CITY

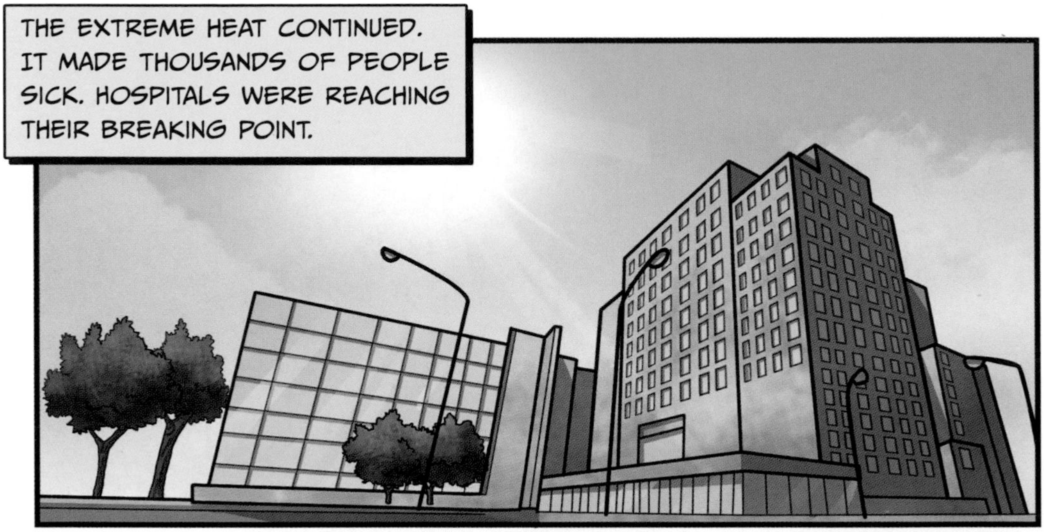
THE EXTREME HEAT CONTINUED. IT MADE THOUSANDS OF PEOPLE SICK. HOSPITALS WERE REACHING THEIR BREAKING POINT.

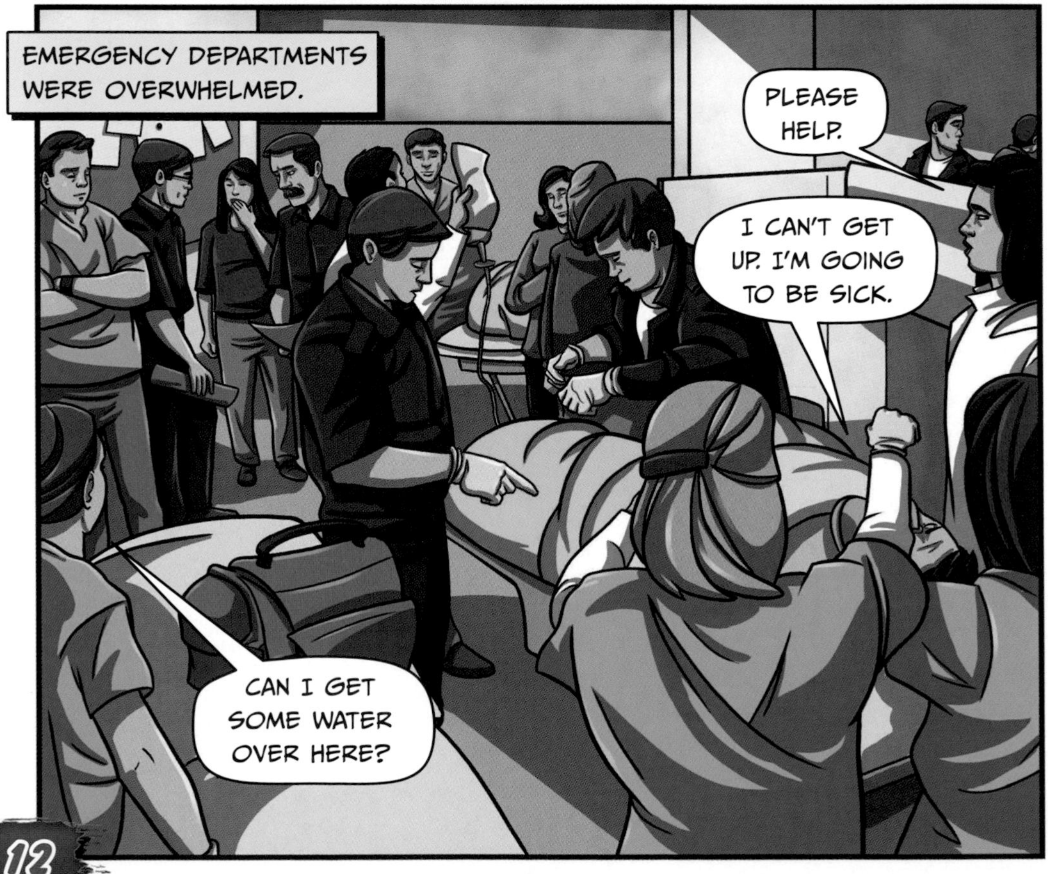
EMERGENCY DEPARTMENTS WERE OVERWHELMED.
PLEASE HELP.
I CAN'T GET UP. I'M GOING TO BE SICK.
CAN I GET SOME WATER OVER HERE?

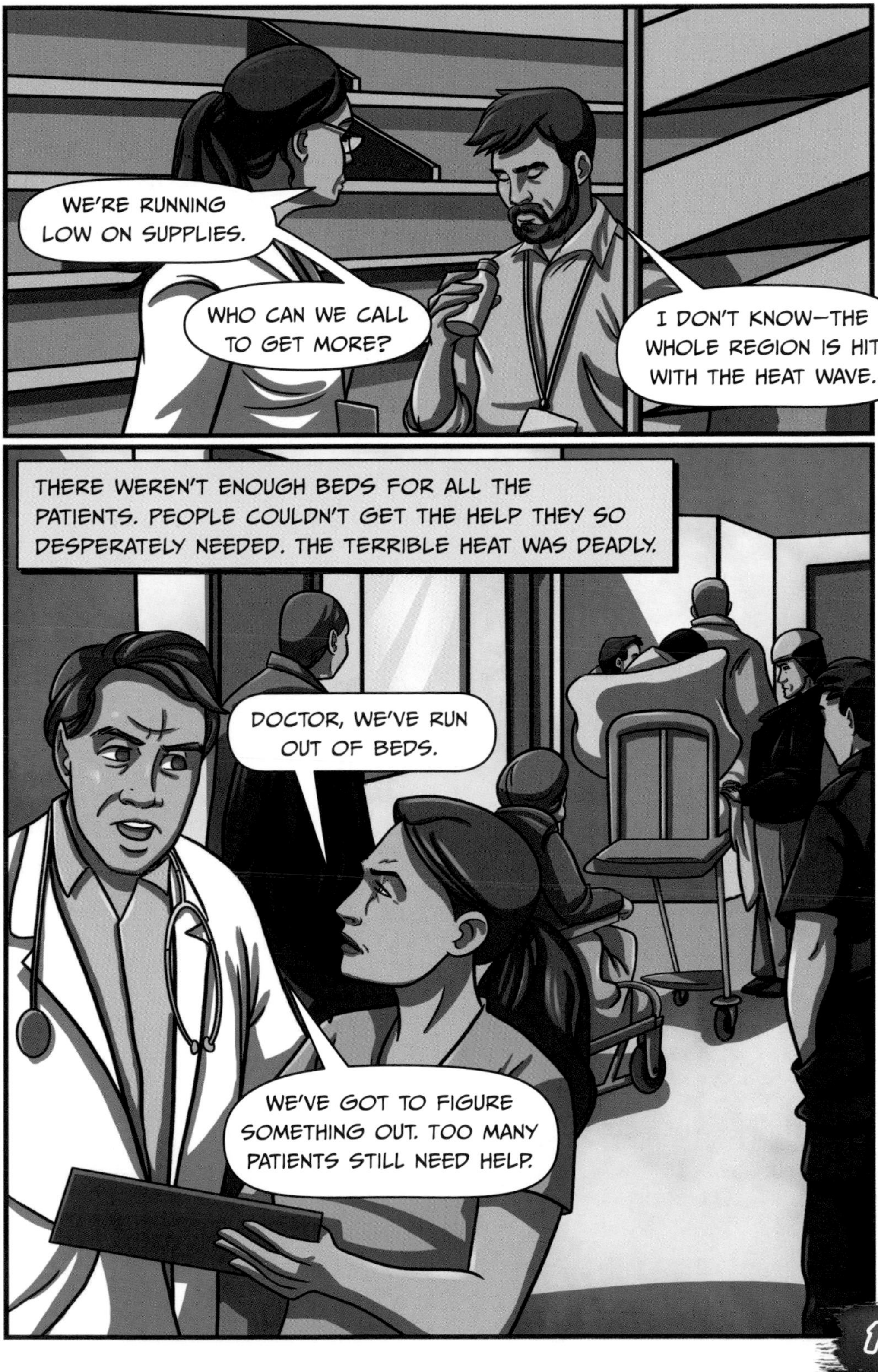
WE'RE RUNNING LOW ON SUPPLIES.
WHO CAN WE CALL TO GET MORE?
I DON'T KNOW—THE WHOLE REGION IS HIT WITH THE HEAT WAVE.
THERE WEREN'T ENOUGH BEDS FOR ALL THE PATIENTS. PEOPLE COULDN'T GET THE HELP THEY SO DESPERATELY NEEDED. THE TERRIBLE HEAT WAS DEADLY.
DOCTOR, WE'VE RUN OUT OF BEDS.
WE'VE GOT TO FIGURE SOMETHING OUT. TOO MANY PATIENTS STILL NEED HELP.

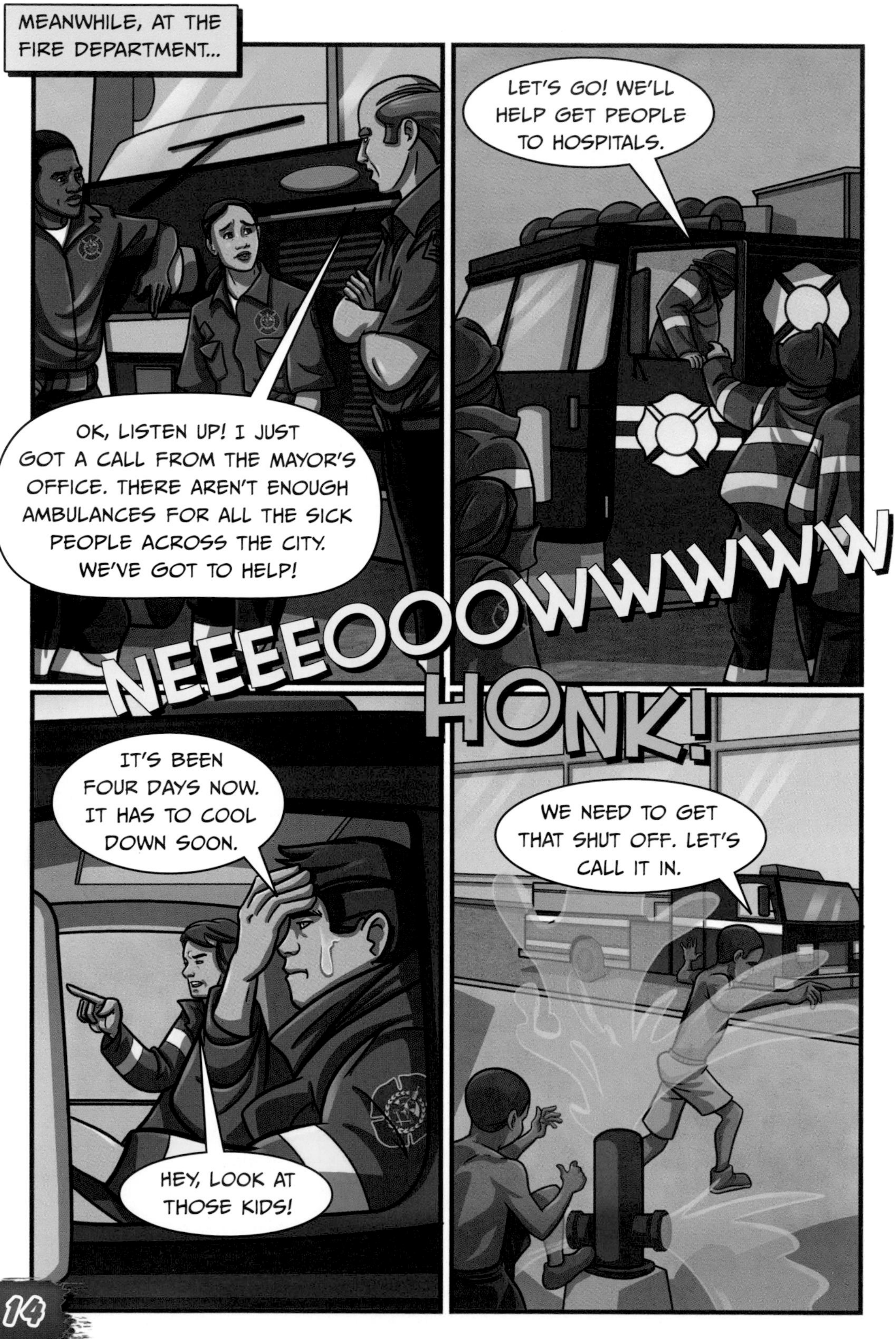
MEANWHILE, AT THE FIRE DEPARTMENT...
OK, LISTEN UP! I JUST GOT A CALL FROM THE MAYOR'S OFFICE. THERE AREN'T ENOUGH AMBULANCES FOR ALL THE SICK PEOPLE ACROSS THE CITY. WE'VE GOT TO HELP!
LET'S GO! WE'LL HELP GET PEOPLE TO HOSPITALS.
NEEEEOOOOWWWWWW
HONK!
IT'S BEEN FOUR DAYS NOW. IT HAS TO COOL DOWN SOON.
HEY, LOOK AT THOSE KIDS!
WE NEED TO GET THAT SHUT OFF. LET'S CALL IT IN.

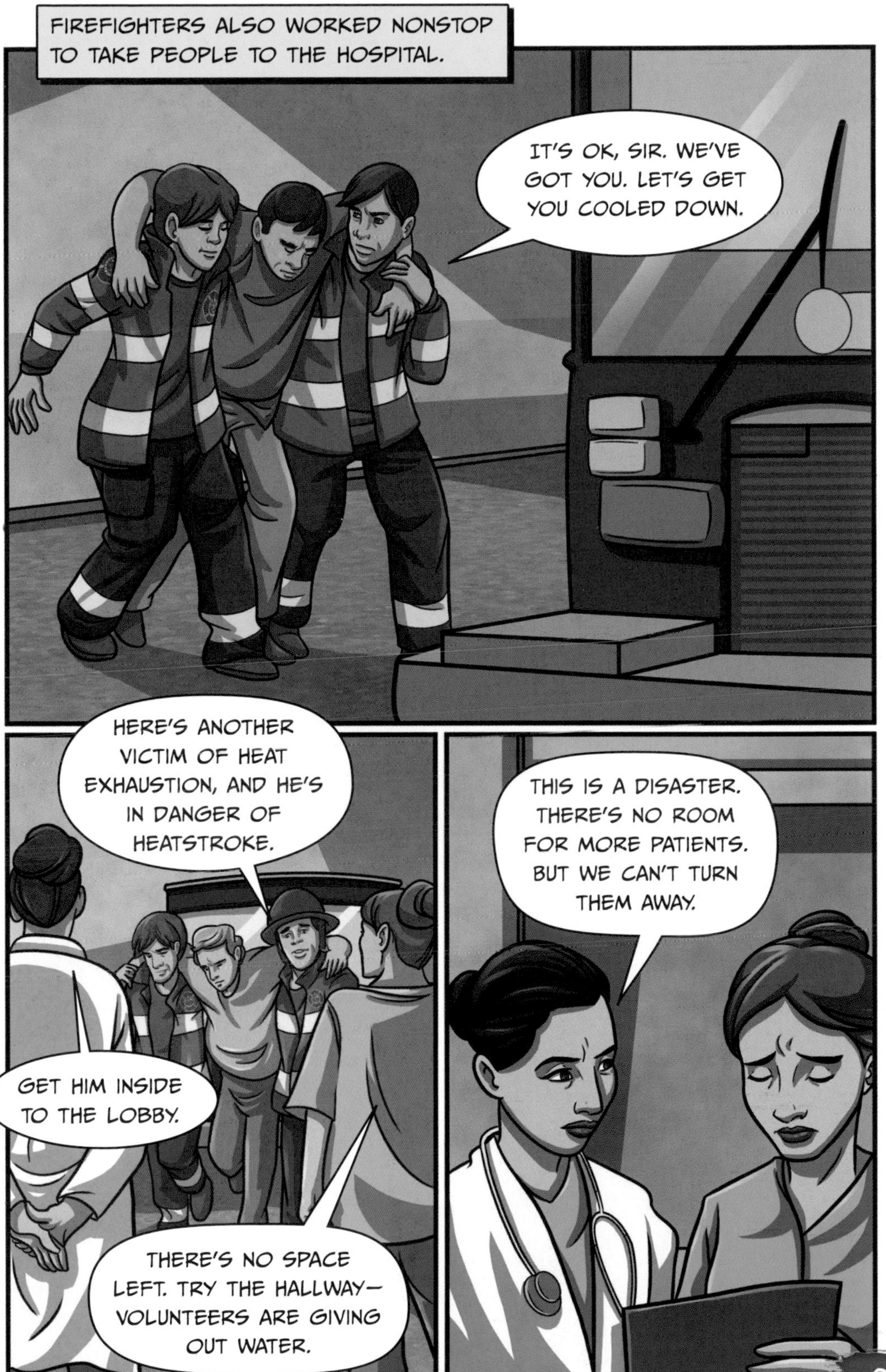
FIREFIGHTERS ALSO WORKED NONSTOP TO TAKE PEOPLE TO THE HOSPITAL.
IT'S OK, SIR. WE'VE GOT YOU. LET'S GET YOU COOLED DOWN.
HERE'S ANOTHER VICTIM OF HEAT EXHAUSTION, AND HE'S IN DANGER OF HEATSTROKE.
GET HIM INSIDE TO THE LOBBY.
THERE'S NO SPACE LEFT. TRY THE HALLWAY—VOLUNTEERS ARE GIVING OUT WATER.
THIS IS A DISASTER. THERE'S NO ROOM FOR MORE PATIENTS. BUT WE CAN'T TURN THEM AWAY.

Chapter 4

HOT ENOUGH TO KILL

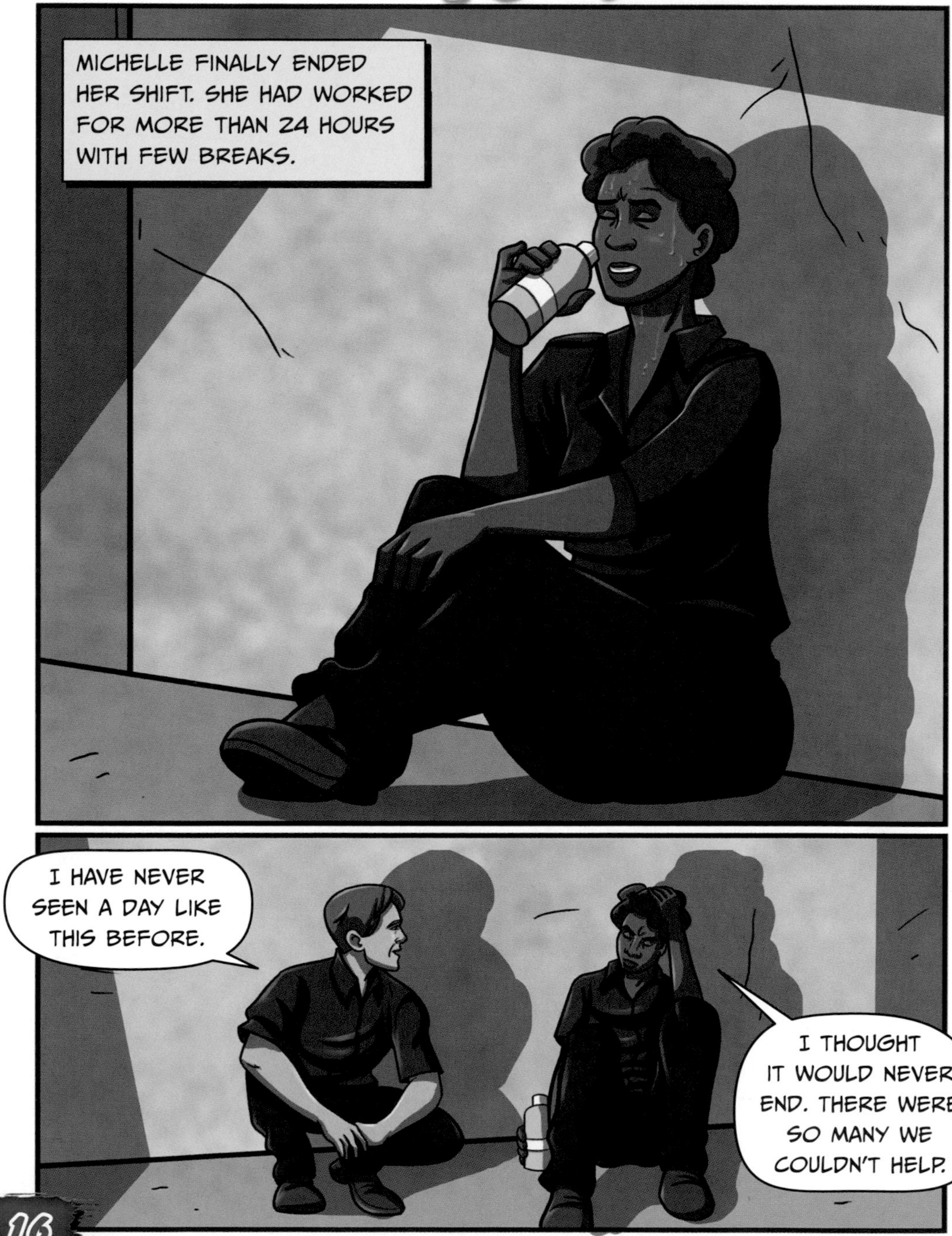
MICHELLE FINALLY ENDED HER SHIFT. SHE HAD WORKED FOR MORE THAN 24 HOURS WITH FEW BREAKS.
I HAVE NEVER SEEN A DAY LIKE THIS BEFORE.
I THOUGHT IT WOULD NEVER END. THERE WERE SO MANY WE COULDN'T HELP.

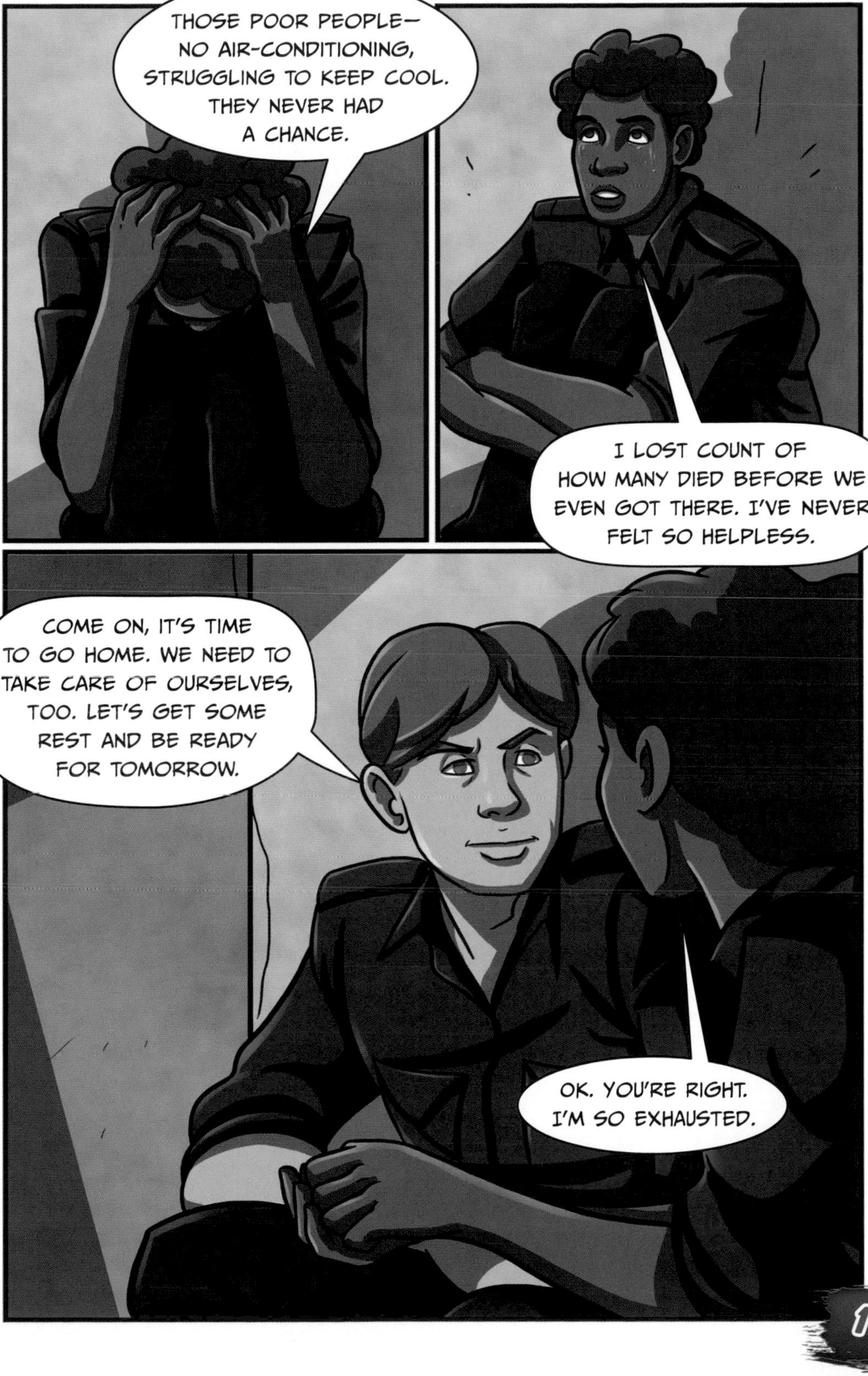
THOSE POOR PEOPLE— NO AIR-CONDITIONING, STRUGGLING TO KEEP COOL. THEY NEVER HAD A CHANCE.
I LOST COUNT OF HOW MANY DIED BEFORE WE EVEN GOT THERE. I'VE NEVER FELT SO HELPLESS.
COME ON, IT'S TIME TO GO HOME. WE NEED TO TAKE CARE OF OURSELVES, TOO. LET'S GET SOME REST AND BE READY FOR TOMORROW.
OK. YOU'RE RIGHT. I'M SO EXHAUSTED.

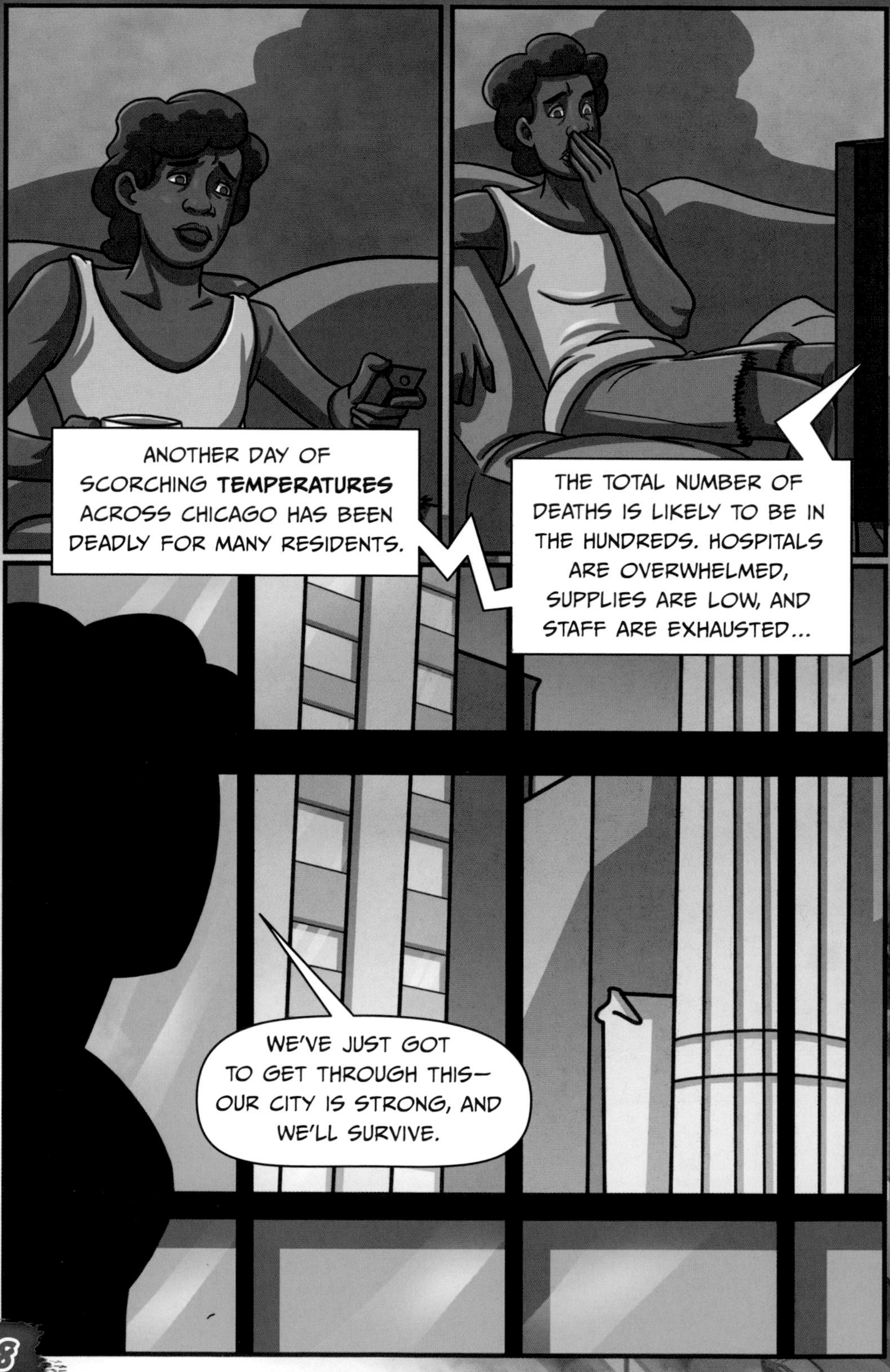
ANOTHER DAY OF SCORCHING **TEMPERATURES** ACROSS CHICAGO HAS BEEN DEADLY FOR MANY RESIDENTS.
THE TOTAL NUMBER OF DEATHS IS LIKELY TO BE IN THE HUNDREDS. HOSPITALS ARE OVERWHELMED, SUPPLIES ARE LOW, AND STAFF ARE EXHAUSTED...
WE'VE JUST GOT TO GET THROUGH THIS— OUR CITY IS STRONG, AND WE'LL SURVIVE.

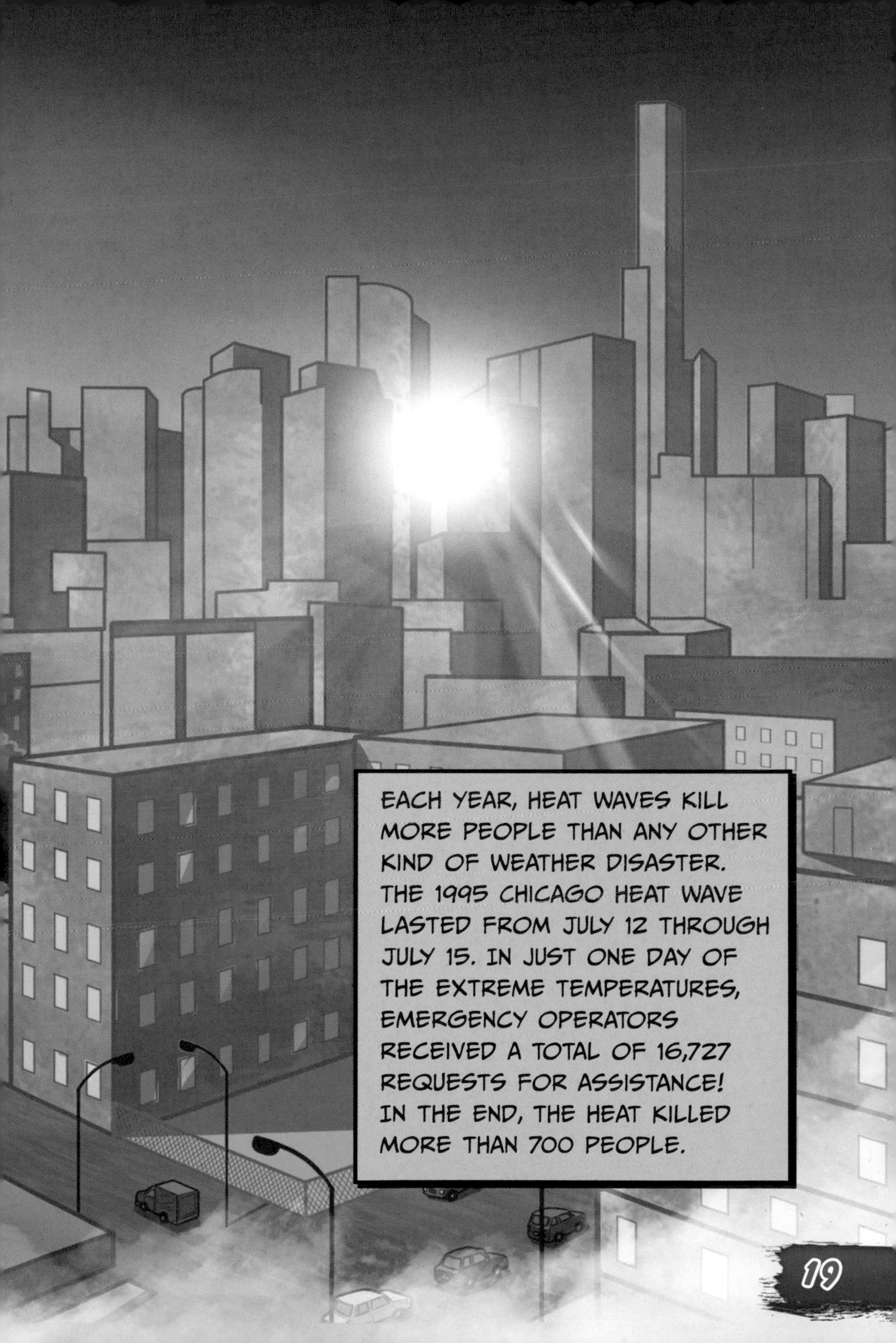
EACH YEAR, HEAT WAVES KILL MORE PEOPLE THAN ANY OTHER KIND OF WEATHER DISASTER. THE 1995 CHICAGO HEAT WAVE LASTED FROM JULY 12 THROUGH JULY 15. IN JUST ONE DAY OF THE EXTREME TEMPERATURES, EMERGENCY OPERATORS RECEIVED A TOTAL OF 16,727 REQUESTS FOR ASSISTANCE! IN THE END, THE HEAT KILLED MORE THAN 700 PEOPLE.

WHAT IS A HEAT WAVE?

Heat waves always occur during the summer when the days are longer and the sun has more time to heat the **atmosphere**.

Sometimes temperatures reach more than 10 degrees Fahrenheit (5 degrees Celsius) above normal. When these high temperatures last for several days in a row, most consider it a heat wave. The hot air stays until winds high in Earth's atmosphere blow it away. Then, temperatures can return to normal.

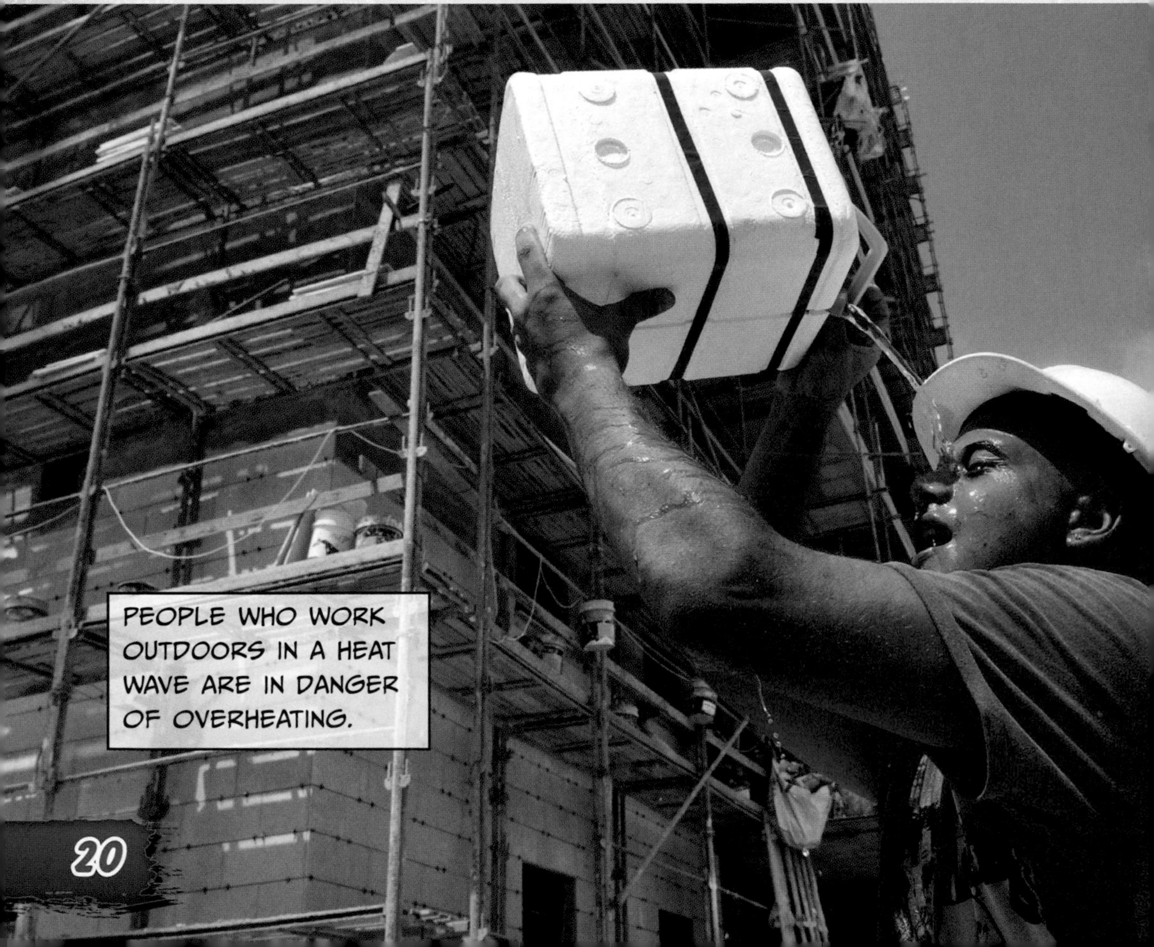

PEOPLE WHO WORK OUTDOORS IN A HEAT WAVE ARE IN DANGER OF OVERHEATING.

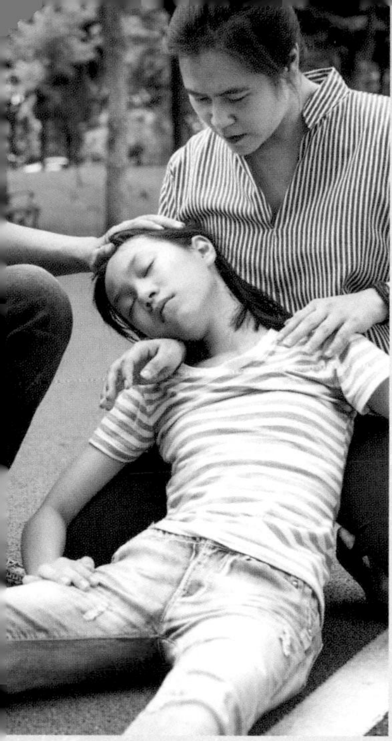

HEATSTROKE

THE NORMALL HUMAN BODY TEMPERATURE IS 98.6°F (37°C). WHEN A PERSON'S BODY IS TOO HOT, IT SWEATS. THIS LIQUID ON THE SKIN **EVAPORATES** AND COOLS THE BODY. IN EXTREME HEAT, SOMETIMES SWEATING IS NOT ENOUGH TO KEEP COOL. WHEN A BODY'S TEMPERATURE REACHES 104°F (40°C) OR HIGHER, HEATSTROKE CAN OCCUR. THIS DANGEROUS CONDITION CAN BE DEADLY.

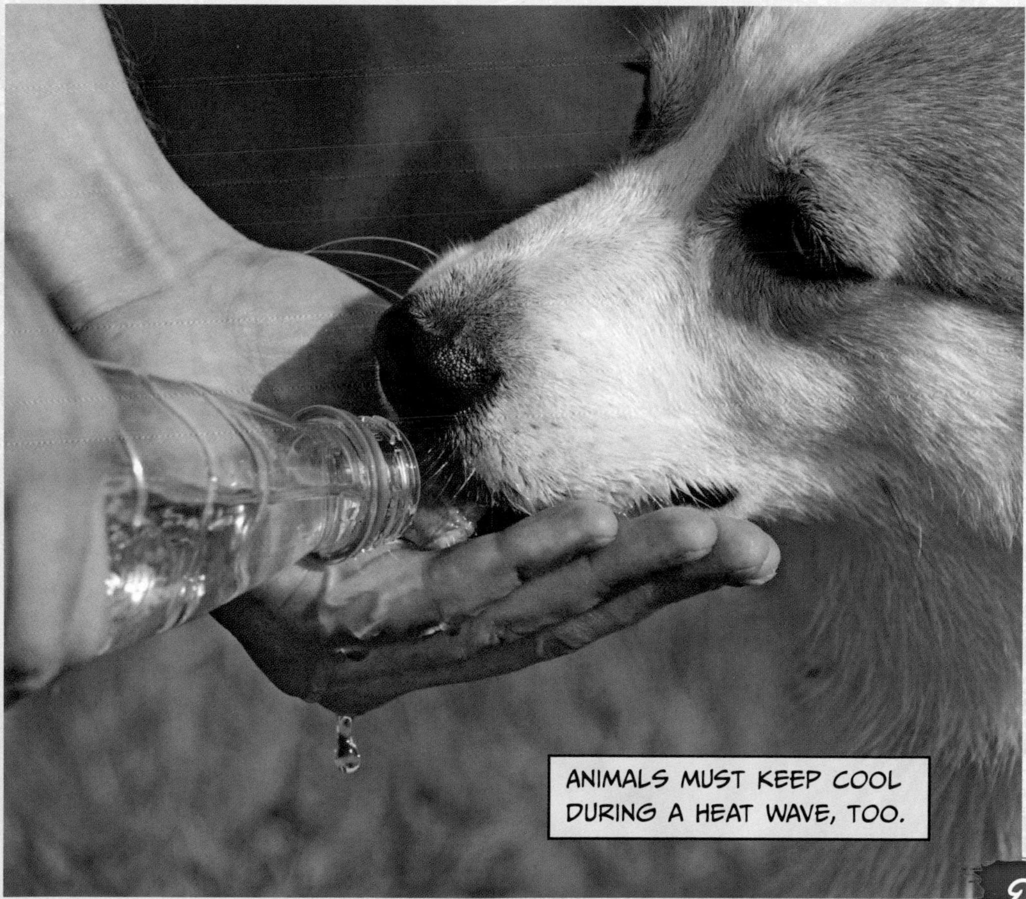

ANIMALS MUST KEEP COOL DURING A HEAT WAVE, TOO.

KEEP SAFE

Here are some heat wave safety tips.

- Stay indoors where you are out of the sun and there is air-conditioning.
- Drink plenty of water, even if you do not feel thirsty.
- Check on elderly neighbors. Older people are most at risk during a heat wave. Their bodies often can not cool themselves as well.
- Do not exercise during the hottest part of the day.
- Never leave a pet or a child alone in a vehicle. The inside of a car can heat up very quickly, even if a window is left open.
- Wear light-colored, loose-fitting clothes. Pale clothes reflect the sun's light and may help you stay cooler. Always wear a hat when you are out in the sun.
- If you do not have air-conditioning, find a cool place near your home. Libraries, shopping malls, and movie theaters are often cool, so consider visiting one of these places during extreme heat.

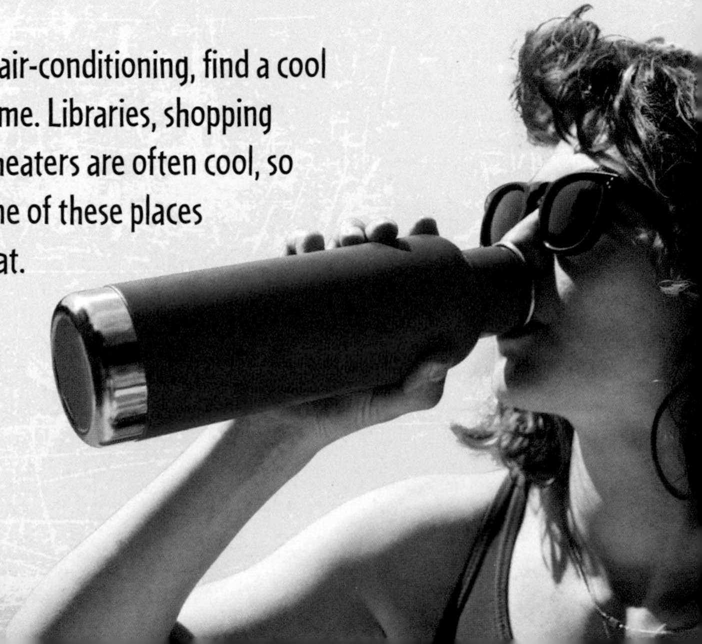

GLOSSARY

air-conditioning a system that controls the temperature in a building or car

atmosphere the layer of gases that surrounds Earth

casualties people who need medical help or who have died

collapsed fallen down from exhaustion or disease

dispatch the people who take calls from the public and then send emergency workers to help

evaporates changes from a liquid into a gas

heatstroke a dangerous condition in which the body becomes too hot to function properly

paramedic a person trained in emergency medical care

sweltering uncomfortably hot

temperatures how hot or cold things are

victim a person who is harmed, injured, or killed

INDEX

air-conditioning 10, 17, 22

ambulances 4, 6, 14

atmosphere 20

casualties 6

Chicago 4, 18-19

dispatch 7, 10

emergency workers 9, 19

fire department 14

firefighters 14-15

heat exhaustion 15

heatstroke 5, 9, 15, 21

hospitals 5, 12, 14-15, 18

paramedics 4, 9

temperatures 18-21

READ MORE

Black, Vanessa. *Heat Waves (Disaster Zone)*. Minneapolis: Jump! (2017).

David, Alexis. *Burning Up: Escalating Heat Waves and Forest Fires (Taking Action on Climate Change)*. New York: Cavendish Square (2020).

Seigel, Rachel. *Heat Wave and Drought Readiness (Natural Disasters: Meeting the Challenge)*. New York: Crabtree (2020).

LEARN MORE ONLINE

1. Go to **www.factsurfer.com**

2. Enter **"Heat Wave Horror"** into the search box.

3. Click on the cover of this book to see a list of websites.